Congratulations!

You've just purchased a cookbook full of

kidney-friendly recipes for smoothies,

snacks and sandwiches to inspire you to live

healthier.

So go on... turn the pages and be inspired!

Thanks ...

to Rhonda, Ruth, Amiee, Diane, Laurie, Kim, Dr. Ruggles and all the hemodialysis techs, nurses, doctors and staff at Davita who work so hard to help my kidneys do their best.

The recipes and tips featured in this book are not intended to be a substitute for professional guidance. While generally suitable for a renal diet, it is important you consult with your dietitian, doctor or nutritionist as to the proper ingredients and portions recommended for your individual health conditions. The author hereby disclaims any absolute reliance on the figures and calculations contained herein.

Original cover art by Brenda Pettitt at brendapettitartist.com and original artwork of author and her dogs by Amiee Lee, a Certified Hemodialysis Technician.

Introduction

The Renal diet can be one of the hardest lifestyle changes for individuals to understand, coordinate (with other diets) and, last but not least, follow over the long term. I was diagnosed with End Stage Renal Disease about 18 months ago, was not successful trying Peritoneal Dialysis and am now on hemodialysis. During this time, I have worked to create a diet plan I can live with and enjoy.

In my first cookbook, *The Renal Survival Cookbook*, I included the best of those recipes and hope that you enjoyed them and have been able to incorporate them into your cooking.

How many days a week do you spend in dialysis? 3? 4? 7? Whatever it is, it's a lot of time. With so many hours of my week dedicated to it, I decided to focus this cookbook on kidney-friendly foods I can munch on while being dialyzed.

Whether you're at the hemodialysis center, using PD at work or at home or running around doing your errands, it enhances your treatment to eat and drink nutritiously... not to simply grab some deadly 'fast food' and eat on the run. I know I'm often too tired to fix up a healthy snack after treatment although I'm hungry, so here are some great ways to do just that –

to make drinks, snacks and sandwiches ahead of time so they are ready when you need them. Make some recipes up, keep them with you to munch and feel better all day long!

Go to your local farmer's market or the produce section in your favorite store and select all the fruits and veggies that you love the most. Better yet, try something new – be inspired to experiment! Or, throw some seeds into pots on your deck and with a little effort grow an endless supply of fresh zucchini, melon, cucumbers, kale and all your favorite veggies and fruits...

You can combine them to create new flavors yourself or make some of these delicious recipes. Remember, the possibilities are practically limitless. Make the most of your own favorite tastes and consistencies (for the smoothies) – and your imagination – to create new drinks and dishes all your own.

Be inspired - feel better every day and fight renal disease with good food!!

Table of Contents

Renal Pantry List

There's nothing as delicious as a home-cooked meal shared by friends and family – or just by you at the end of a long day. Cooking kidney-friendly recipes are not only good for your health, but they can also serve to bring everyone together for great food and healthy drinks. Keep these 100 kidney-friendly ingredients in your pantry so you can whip up a tasty meal or smoothie whenever you're in the mood!

When you get the cooking bug, you're going to want to get as good at it as you can and make your food just delicious as quickly as possible.

To do that you'll need the right kitchen equipment, plenty of practice and a cupboard full of good basic ingredients. All that stuff that sits in your cupboard or freezer waiting for you to come home and cook, is really important because that's what makes your food taste great and good for your kidneys.

If you buy yourself a nice piece of cod, beef or chicken, you can take it to Spain, Italy, India or China just by using certain herbs or spices from your cupboards. That's what's so exciting about cooking.

It's good to remember that there's nothing substandard about canned tomatoes, canned tuna or canned and frozen fruits and vegetables. Things like frozen peas are picked at their best and preserved that way until you use them. Unless you're picking them from your garden, you'll have to go a long way to get a tastier and more nutritional pea than a frozen one.

The moral of the story is: Use the list. Go and buy it all. It won't cost the earth, and it's not going to go bad. It will sit happily in your cupboard or freezer for months. Having these basics will allow you to do more exciting things with your food – to be inspired to experiment. The truth is, there should be enough in your pantry to get you out of trouble if you get snowed in...so stock up!

General Dry Goods

1. All-purpose flour
2. Spelt flour
3. Baking powder
4. Cream of tartar
5. Cornstarch
6. Dried yeast
7. Superfine sugar
8. Confectioner's sugar
9. Sugar substitute (Splenda, etc.)
10. Chow mein noodles
11. Vanilla extract
12. Evaporated non-fat milk

13. Cereal (corn and rice)
14. Oatmeal
15. Cream of Wheat
16. Dried fruit (apricots, cranberries, etc.)

Nutritional

18. Dulce flakes
19. Spirulena
20. Protein Powder

Frozen

21. Peas
22. Sugar snap peas
23. Green beans
24. Sweet corn
25. Fruits
26. Raw shrimp
27. Frozen pesto cubes
28. *Frozen kale cubes*

Herbs & Spices

30. Basil
31. Thyme
32. Oregano
33. Marjoram
34. Rosemary
35. Sage
36. Parsley
37. Savory

38. Coriander
39. Garlic
40. Garlic powder
41. Onion powder
42. Cloves, ground
43. Allspice
44. Nutmeg
45. Ginger, ground
46. Cinnamon
47. Cumin
48. Black pepper
49. Dill
50. Bay leaves
51. Chili powder
52. Dry mustard
53. Kosher salt

Canned & Jarred Goods

54. Chicken, beef & vegetable broth
55. Canned coconut milk
56. Vegetable broth
57. Pumpkin puree
58. Applesauce
59. Canned fruits and vegetables
60. Soup
61. Canned meats (tuna, chicken, etc.)
62. Pesto

Pasta & Grains

63. Rice

64. Quick-cook couscous
65. Dried pasta (spaghetti, elbow, lasagna, etc.)
66. Lentils
67. Popcorn

Snacks

68. Pretzels/ Veggie Chips
69. Crackers, unsalted

Condiments

70. Ketchup
71. Dijon mustard
72. Honey
73. Mayonnaise
74. Salad dressing
75. Barbeque sauce
76. Sweet chili sauce
77. Soy sauce
78. Worcestershire sauce
79. Hot sauce
80. Maple syrup
81. White vinegar
82. Apple cider vinegar
83. Balsamic vinegar
84. Wine vinegar
85. Pickles
86. Jam / Jelly
87. Molasses

Fats / Oils

88. Extra-virgin olive oil
89. Sesame oil
90. White wine vinegar
91. Canola oil
92. Red-wine vinegar
93. Balsamic vinegar
94. Grapeseed oil

Drinks

95. Coffee
96. Tea
97. Apple juice
98. Grape juice
99. Ginger-ale & 7Up
100. Lemonade drink mix

Renal Smoothies

In order to get my daily requirement of fruits and vegetables without spending hours on end chewing salads or worrying about keeping my labs good (maintaining healthy Potassium, Phosphorous levels, etc.), I have devised a delicious way to cheat... Renal Smoothies. I'm addicted!!

For anyone new to eating vegetables and/or fruits, start slowly to integrate smoothies in your diet as they have been known to make even the most devoted vegan make a face, but the health benefits can't be ignored. I started drinking these about a year ago, and have actually grown to like them (most of the time that is, but I tolerate them now and love them because of how great I feel).

I have noticed a huge increase in energy, skin improvement, and hair growing faster as well as better sleep since adding them to my diet. There are plenty of benefits that you will get from just simply enjoying smoothies in addition to helping your kidneys. If you blend veggies and fruits you can obtain the vitamins that your body needs to stay healthy. Dietary fibers also help expel dangerous compounds and substances from our bodies such as carcinogens. If you want to slim down, you can include drinking green smoothies for your diet as they assist in cleansing substances that are not essential for your body. All I could say is definitely green or fruit smoothies are the best substitute for daily beverages. So why not start drinking smoothies instead of unhealthy sodas? Not only are they natural but also they are much healthier and cheaper than the beverages that we usually drink. Purchase the ingredients to make your favorite smoothies right now and start enjoying their healthy and long-lasting benefits. And you'll never have leftovers again!

Here's the way I make my smoothies... you can use it as your general guide – but remember to experiment!!!

- ➤ Start by adding the liquid (rice milk, apple juice, coconut milk, etc.) to your blender,
- ➤ Followed by a thickener if your recipe calls for it (yogurt, tofu, frozen yogurt, sorbet, ice, etc.),
- ➤ Followed by the soft or frozen fruit and veggies...
- ➤ Add the greens to your blender last...

- ➢ Blend on high for 30 seconds or until the smoothie has reached the consistency you prefer.
- ➢ Enjoy any time of day or night!!

Liquid	Thickener	Fruits/Veggies	Extras
		Fresh, frozen or canned in juice	*Your choice…*
Rice milk, apple juice, coconut milk, etc.	Yogurt, tofu, sorbet, ice, sherbet, etc.	Strawberries, blueberries, peaches, kale, carrots, celery, cucumber, etc.	Spirulina, dulse flakes, honey, preserves, etc.

I've developed a basic renal green smoothie recipe that includes some combination of the top 15 kidney-friendly super foods according to Davita.com. These foods are good for everyone, not just people with kidney disease, so by using them in your family's meals, you'll be helping everyone enjoy good health too.

Basic Renal Green Smoothie

In your blender, combine:

- ✓ ½ small tomato
- ✓ 1/3 of a cucumber
- ✓ ½ red bell pepper
- ✓ ½ cup cauliflower
- ✓ 2 green apples

- ✓ 1 cup grapes
- ✓ ½ cup red cabbage
- ✓ 1 jalapeno
- ✓ ¼ of an onion
- ✓ 1-2 cloves of raw garlic
- ✓ 1-2 stalks of celery
- ✓ 3-4 big handfuls of greens of choice (kale, lettuce, spinach)
- ✓ 1 Tsp. dulse flakes
- ✓ 1 Tsp. Spirulina
- ✓ Salt & pepper to taste
- ✓ 1-2 cups water (depending on the thickness you prefer)
- ✓ Handful of ice cubes

Here's a quick primer on the benefits of these ingredients:

- ➤ Tomatoes - Full of lycopene, Vitamin C, Vitamin A, Potassium, and antioxidants – because of their high Potassium content, use sparingly and be sure to consult your renal dietician.
- ➤ Cucumber - High water content, Vitamin C, silica, caffeic acid, potassium, and magnesium.
- ➤ Celery - Vitamins A, B2, B6 and C, Potassium, Folic Acid, Magnesium and Calcium.
- ➤ Red Bell Peppers - Vitamin C, Thiamine, Vitamin B6, Beta Carotene, Folic Acid and a variety of phytochemicals while low in potassium.
- ➤ Onions - Beneficial sulfur containing compounds, Vitamin C, Chromium,

manganese, can help lower blood sugar, reduce cancer risk and lower cholesterol. Low in potassium, onions are not only kidney-friendly; they also contain chromium, a mineral that assists your body with the metabolism of fats, proteins and carbohydrates.

➢ Greens - Combination of spinach, kale, mustard greens, lettuce and green herbs containing a wide variety of nutrients and beneficial compounds.

➢ Jalapenos - Capsaicin, Vitamin C and other. Can help relieve headache, congestion, high blood pressure, inflammation, intestinal diseases as well as aid weight loss and strengthen the heart.

➢ Kelp or Dulse Flakes - Great source of Iodine and trace minerals. Dulse is a red seaweed, or algae, that is native to the North Atlantic Ocean. It is used both as food and medicine. The dried seaweed can be broken into small flakes that are used in cooking and in your smoothies.

➢ Spirulina - A green-blue cyanobacteria. Great source of protein, good immune support and the most nutrient dense whole food.

➢ Cabbage - Crunchy cabbage is a cruciferous vegetable filled with phytochemicals, chemical compounds found in certain fruits and vegetables. Phytochemicals work to break apart free radicals. Many phytochemicals are believed to combat cancer and support cardiovascular health. Inexpensive cabbage is a great addition to your eating plan, because it's also high in vitamins K and C, high in fiber and a good source of vitamin B6 and folic acid, yet it's low in potassium, so it's especially kidney-friendly.

➤ Cauliflower - Another kidney-friendly super food this cruciferous vegetable brings lots of vitamin C to your plate, along with folate and fiber. In addition it contains compounds that help your liver neutralize toxic substances.

➤ Garlic - is good for reducing inflammation and lowering cholesterol. It also has antioxidant and anti-clotting properties, Immune support, anti-cancer and infection fighting properties.

➤ Egg whites/Tofu (silken style for added smoothness)-Did you know that egg whites are pure protein? They provide the highest quality protein there is, along with all of the essential amino acids. If you're on the kidney diet, it's good to note that egg whites have less phosphorus than other protein sources, such as egg yolks or meats.

Basic Renal Fruit Smoothie

In your blender, combine:

- ✓ 2 small apples
- ✓ ½ of a cucumber
- ✓ ½ cup frozen red grapes
- ✓ ½ cup frozen blackberries/raspberries
- ✓ ½ cup frozen blueberries
- ✓ ½ cup frozen cranberries

- ✓ ½ cup pineapple
- ✓ ¾ cup non-fat yogurt
- ✓ ½ cup silken tofu
- ✓ 1 Tsp. dulse flakes
- ✓ 1 Tsp. Spirulina
- ✓ handful of ice cubes (depending upon your thickness preference)

Here's a quick primer on the benefits of these ingredients:

- ➤ Kelp or Dulse Flakes - Great source of Iodine and trace minerals. Dulse is a red seaweed, or algae, that is native to the North Atlantic Ocean. It is used both as food and medicine. The dried seaweed can be broken into small flakes that are used in cooking and in your smoothies.
- ➤ Spirulina - A green-blue cyanobacteria. Great source of protein, good immune support and the most nutrient dense whole food
- ➤ Apples - High in fiber and anti-inflammatory properties, apples help reduce cholesterol, prevent constipation, protect against heart disease and decrease your risk of cancer.
- ➤ Cranberries - Are great for preventing urinary tract infections, because they make urine more acidic and help keep bacteria from attaching to the inside of the bladder. They've also been shown to protect against cancer and heart disease.
- ➤ Blueberries - These tasty berries get their blue color from antioxidant compounds called anthocyanidins. Blueberries get high marks

for nutrition, thanks to natural compounds that reduce inflammation and lots of vitamin C and fiber. They also contain manganese, which contributes to healthy bones.

➤ Raspberries - Contain a compound called ellagic acid, which helps neutralize free radicals. The berry's red color comes from antioxidants called anthocyanins. Raspberries are packed with fiber, vitamin C and manganese. They also have plenty of folate, a B vitamin. Raspberries have properties that help stop cancer cell growth and the formation of tumors.

➤ Strawberries - Are rich in two types of antioxidants, plus they contain lots of vitamin C, manganese and fiber. They have anti-inflammatory and anti-cancer properties and also help keep your heart healthy.

➤ Cherries - Are filled with antioxidants and phytochemicals that protect your heart. When eaten daily, they have been shown to reduce inflammation.

➤ Red grapes - The color in red grapes comes from several flavonoids. These are good for your heart, because they prevent oxidation and reduce the chance of blood clots. One flavonoid in grapes, resveratrol, may boost production of nitric oxide, which increases muscle relaxation in blood vessels for better blood flow. Flavonoids also help protect you from cancer and prevent inflammation. Choose those with red or purple skin grapes for the highest flavonoid content. Eat grapes as a snack. When frozen, they make a good thirst-quencher for those on a fluid-restricted diet.

➢ Egg whites/Tofu (silken style for added smoothness) - Did you know that egg whites are pure protein? They provide the highest quality protein there is, along with all of the essential amino acids. If you're on the kidney diet, it's good to note that egg whites have less phosphorus than other protein sources, such as egg yolks or meats.

I make my smoothies in our Ninja (with a 72 oz. pitcher), so quantities might need to be adjusted if you have a smaller size blender. If you don't have all the ingredients, use what you do have and add any vegetables or fruits that can be eaten raw.

Blend all the ingredients until smooth. It should be thick – but you can control that by adding ice if it's too heavy. I find the easiest way to drink one is to take 3 gulps and then give it a rest. Put it back in the refrigerator or tighten up your smoothie glass if you're taking your smoothie on the road or to dialysis.

☼ *Quick Tips & Tricks*

When using your blender, for best results:

✓ Quickly pulse 3-4 times to help break up any recipes that use ice. The harder the ingredients, the more pulses you'll need.

✓ Quick pulsing is the best method to process foods. Pulse similarly textured foods together for better consistency.

✓ Pulp is the healthiest part of any juice - providing you with the most nutrition.

✓ If you prefer less pulp, add more water based fruits and vegetables like melon and cucumber. The longer you blend, the smother it gets.

Immunize Me! Juice

"Green smoothies taste great and will boost your nutrition and energy levels. They're so quick and simple to make – all you need is a good blender like a VitaMix, Ninja, or Cuisinart – something with enough power to blend all the ingredients well. Take your smoothie with you to dialysis or keep it in the fridge and grab a mouthful or two throughout the day as a refreshing snack.

This green smoothie will also help keep your levels of potassium in check. Potassium supports heart, muscle and cognitive function. Renal disease may reduce your kidney's ability to manage potassium and lead to excessive levels of the mineral. To prevent complications of high potassium levels, such as rapid *heartbeat, your doctor may suggest a low-potassium diet.*

Foods rich in potassium include fruits, such as lima beans, bananas, oranges, cantaloupe, raisins, apricots, broccoli, potatoes, tomatoes, Swiss chard, mustard greens, mushrooms, chocolate, salt substitute, nuts, coffee and chocolate.

Nutritious low-potassium alternatives include apples, green beans, grapes, pears, watermelon, cranberries, carrots, cucumbers, onions, lettuce, cherries, rice, noodles, breads and cereals. Because most foods contain some potassium, the Medical College of Wisconsin recommends learning and adhering to appropriate portion sizes."

INGREDIENTS

- ✓ 2 green apples, quartered & seeded
- ✓ 4 cucumbers
- ✓ 1" piece ginger root
- ✓ 1 lemon, quartered
- ✓ 8 Romaine lettuce leaves

PREPARATION

1. Mix all ingredients in your blender until you achieve the desired consistency.
2. Enjoy!

Raspberry Smoothies

"Raspberries are very high in antioxidants and also contain high levels of fiber, manganese and vitamin C. Other nutrients in raspberries include vitamins B1-3, folic acid, magnesium, copper and iron.

Raspberries have anti-inflammatory properties. Studies suggest that eating raspberries may prevent certain cancers and protect against cardiovascular disease, diabetes, allergies, age-related cognitive decline and macular degeneration (age-related vision problems).

And they're just delicious any way you serve them!"

Raspberry-Apple Smoothie

- ✓ 1 cup raspberries
- ✓ 1 apple
- ✓ 1 pear
- ✓ 2 cups fresh baby spinach (or other leafy green)
- ✓ 1 carrot
- ✓ ½ – 1 cup water

Raspberry-Watermelon Smoothie

- ✓ 1 cup raspberries
- ✓ 2 cups watermelon
- ✓ 1 banana
- ✓ 2 cups fresh baby spinach (or other leafy green)
- ✓ 1 celery stalk
- ✓ ½ cup water if needed

Black Raspberry-Banana Smoothie

- ✓ ½ cup of red raspberries
- ✓ ½ cup of blackberries
- ✓ 1 whole banana
- ✓ ¼ cup of silken tofu
- ✓ 2 cups fresh baby spinach (or other leafy green)
- ✓ ½ – 1 cup water

Raspberry & Mint Lemonade

- ✓ 8 oz. club soda
- ✓ ½ cup lemonade
- ✓ ½ cup fresh raspberries
- ✓ 2 Tbsp. powdered sugar
- ✓ 4 mint leaves

Raspberry / Blackberry Burst

- ✓ 1 cup frozen raspberries
- ✓ 1 cup frozen blackberries
- ✓ 1 cup frozen blueberries
- ✓ ½ cup fresh strawberries
- ✓ ¾ cup nonfat yogurt
- ✓ 1 cup orange juice

☼ *Quick Tips & Tricks*

While fresh smoothies can be a healthful snack or breakfast on the go, you can even freeze them for homemade popsicles!

Ginger Smoothies

"Ginger has a variety of health benefits and has been used medicinally for centuries. It's widely known for its immune-boosting and stomach-settling abilities (ie; drinking ginger-ale to settle your stomach). It has been shown to be effective in treating nausea which is often an issue for kidney patients. Some studies suggest that ginger can help relieve intestinal gas and speed up digestion.

Ginger is, however, a mild chemical irritant, so don't go crazy with it in your smoothie recipes. A little bit goes a long way. Ginger ads a warming, spicy flavor to fruit and green smoothies. I find that fresh ginger works best with pineapple and other citrus fruits like orange, lemon and lime. It also blends well with sweet banana or vanilla bean and can be combined with other spices like nutmeg and cinnamon if you like."

Pumpkin Pie Green Smoothie

- ✓ ½ cup organic pumpkin pie mix
- ✓ 1 cup unsweetened, almond milk
- ✓ 1 teaspoon ground cinnamon
- ✓ ½ teaspoon nutmeg
- ✓ 1 large carrot, chopped
- ✓ 2 cups fresh baby spinach (or other leafy green)
- ✓ 2 frozen bananas
- ✓ 1" peeled fresh ginger

Carrot-Apple-Ginger Green Smoothie

- ✓ 2 medium carrots, chopped
- ✓ 1 medium apple, cored
- ✓ 2 large handfuls of baby spinach
- ✓ 1 tablespoon freshly grated ginger root
- ✓ 4 to 6 ounces of filtered water
- ✓ ½" peeled fresh ginger

Pineapple-Vanilla Smoothie

- ✓ 1 cup pineapple
- ✓ 1 banana
- ✓ 1/2 vanilla bean (or more to taste)
- ✓ 2 cups fresh baby spinach (or other leafy green)
- ✓ 1 celery stalk
- ✓ 1/2 – 1 cup water
- ✓ ½" peeled fresh ginger

Hot & Spicy Smoothie

"Here's an experimental smoothie I came up with that is made with no sweet fruit. That's right – no bananas, mangos or pineapple – just vegetables! I was actually surprised how tasty this was. In fact, I've been drinking this savory smoothie (and variations of it) daily for the past two weeks.

Non-sweet fruit and veggies are lower in calories then sweet fruit, so this makes quite a large (42 ounce) smoothie for only 300-400 calories. A smoothie this size isn't too much for me to drink, but it might be a bit overwhelming if you're not used to it. And you need to be sure you factor the fluids into your daily intake goals along with the potassium intake from the tomatoes.

If you can't drink that much all at once, you can cut the recipe in half or make the whole thing and drink half now and half later. Just beware that it'll be a low calorie smoothie.

This smoothie will provide you with all your vegetable needs for the day and then some and may just put a little extra kick in your step!"

INGREDIENTS

- ✓ 8 organic vine tomatoes
- ✓ 2 large organic red bell peppers
- ✓ 1 organic zucchini
- ✓ 2 or 3 onion slices (I used white onion)
- ✓ 8 large organic celery stalks
- ✓ 1 teaspoon flax seeds
- ✓ 1/2 teaspoon dulse flakes
- ✓ 1 tablespoon chili powder
- ✓ dash of cayenne pepper
- ✓ 1/4 avocado (optional to thicken)

PREPARATION

Blend the tomatoes on high until mixed. This will give you enough liquid to mix the rest of the smoothie since I recommend not adding water to it. Add the peppers and zucchini and blend until mixed. Finally, add the remaining ingredients and blend for 30 seconds or until smooth.

☼ Quick Tips & Tricks

You can add a small clove of garlic to this and it's quite tasty. Of course, you can make this smoothie non-spicy by leaving out the chili powder and cayenne and using your favorite herbs instead. Dill, oregano, parsley and cilantro would be delicious. Or try a twist of lemon...

Veggie Smoothies

"Now that you are integrating your favorite homemade smoothies and protein shakes into your renal diet, why not add superfood Kale to your ingredient repertoire and take your smoothies to the next level? Blend kale with immune-boosting fruit to make a sweet smoothie strong enough to fight off the cold and flu season...

Raw kale can enhance any smoothie by adding an impressive 206% of the daily requirement of vitamin A, 134% of vitamin C, and 684% of vitamin K. Fruits like strawberries provide an additional vitamin C boost as well as a great amount of folate, potassium, manganese, and fiber. And, if you use a base like non-fat or low-fat Greek yogurt or silken tofu, it can provide you with up to 22 grams of protein per serving. All while tasting delicious... for anyone in the family!"

INGREDIENTS

Pineapple-Zucchini Smoothie

- ✓ 1 medium organic zucchini
- ✓ 1/2 cup organic Italian (flat-leaf) parsley
- ✓ 2 stalks organic celery
- ✓ 1 cup chopped pineapple
- ✓ 1/3 cup silken tofu
- ✓ 4 to 6 ounces water

Kale Smoothie with Strawberries

- ✓ 1 tightly packed cup of kale, washed and chopped
- ✓ 1 cup of fresh or frozen strawberries
- ✓ 1 cup of non-fat or low-fat vanilla Greek yogurt
- ✓ up to 1 cup of ice

Cucumber Blast

- ✓ 2 grapefruits, peeled and quartered
- ✓ 2 oranges, peeled and quartered
- ✓ ½ cucumber, peeled
- ✓ 4-6 ice cubes

☼ Quick Tips & Tricks

Have some extra fresh kale leftover and worried that you won't use it up before it spoils? Just blend the leftover greens with a little water, pour into an ice cube tray, and freeze! Now you have nutritious kale cubes to quickly pop in the blender for your next smoothie, defrost to make a nourishing juice, or add a boost to your favorite soup.   Delicious!

Fresh Fruit & Veggie

Spritzes

"*Whether you're looking for something new and different to help celebrate a special occasion or just a great pick-me-up on a sluggish day, enjoy the sparkling bubbly effects of these delicious drinks.*

Try substituting ginger ale with Presecco for that special occasion. Prosecco is one of the less-alcoholic sparkling wines, with an alcohol content of just 11%."

INGREDIENTS

Fresh Carrot-Orange-Lemon Spritz

- ✓ 4 carrots
- ✓ 2 oranges
- ✓ 1" fresh ginger, peeled
- ✓ 1 lemon
- ✓ 1 cup ginger ale

Cover a small plate with cane sugar. Rub four glass rims with orange peel and dip lightly into sugar to coat. Juice ingredients (except the ginger ale) in your blender and pour into a pitcher. Stir in 1 cup ginger ale. Serves 4. Simply delicious!

Meyer Lemon Punch Spritz

- ✓ 2 cups brewed black tea
- ✓ ½ cup fresh Meyer lemon juice
- ✓ ¼ cup cane sugar (or sugar substitute)
- ✓ 2 sprigs of fresh rosemary
- ✓ 1 ¼ cups ginger ale

Combine all the ingredients (except for the ginger ale and rosemary) in a pitcher and stir thoroughly until sugar is fully dissolved. Add ginger ale and serve over ice with lemon wedges and rosemary sprigs. Smells and tastes out of this world!

Passion Fruit Float Spritzer

- ✓ ¼ cup passion fruit sorbet
- ✓ ½ cup ginger ale
- ✓ Lime zest

Scoop sorbet into a glass. Slowly top with ginger ale and garnish with lime zest. Caution – easily addictive – in your favorite sorbet flavors!

Blender Ice Creams

& Sorbets

Fruit'N Cream Ice Cream

- ✓ 2 cups frozen fruit (mixed berries, strawberries, peaches, grapes, apples, mangoes, pineapple or whatever you desire – use your imagination and try all kinds of combinations)
- ✓ ½ cup Rice milk cream (or whatever type of milk cream substitute you like best)
- ✓ 2-4 Tbsp. sugar

- ✓ 1 Tsp. vanilla extract

This is a great basic recipe to use your blender to make one of my favorite snacks – ice cream! Place all the ingredients in the pitcher and blend until you've achieved a soft-serve thickness – usually about a minute or two.

Coconut Pineapple Sorbet

- ✓ 1 small ripe pineapple, peeled, cored, roughly cut into 1" pieces and frozen
- ✓ 1 Tbsp. fresh lime juice
- ✓ ½ cup light coconut milk
- ✓ ½ cup super fine sugar
- ✓ 1 Tsp. fresh ginger, chopped

Yogurt & Fruit Ice Cream

- ✓ 1 ½ cups nonfat Greek yogurt
- ✓ 1/3 cup granulates sugar (or substitute as your diet requires)
- ✓ 10-12 ounces frozen fruit
- ✓

☼ Quick Tips & Tricks

For best results, I recommend placing the frozen fruit and the yogurt mixture alternately in layers, starting and ending with the frozen fruit into your blender. Pulse 10 – 15 times until the fruit is broken down. Then process for 35 – 45 seconds until the desired texture is achieved.

Snacks

Munching something delicious is not only a great way to enjoy dialysis treatments, but can also just make you feel good. Being happy is one of the very best ways to improve your health and is often a resolution we make at the beginning of a new year or when tragedy hits – such as being diagnosed with kidney disease.

Clinical psychologist Laura Delizonna, PhD, is teaching a four-course series for the Stanford University Continuing Studies program that focuses on building the fundamental internal skills for happiness and success. She believes that sustainable happiness is a cause, not merely a consequence, of success. In the January 28, 2013 issue of *Inside Stanford Medicine*, Dr. Delizonna answered 5 questions one of which I would like to share with you because I think it's such a good tip to help anyone having to deal with a renal diet...

Q. What are some examples of science-based methods to increase happiness?

A. *Research shows that the simple process of writing down or discussing the positive events that happen each day can provide a significant happiness boost.*

In these studies, people who recorded three good things that happened each day for one week had higher levels of happiness and lower levels of depression. It is thought that this technique trains the mind to scan for what is right, not wrong, in life. When clients I work with use this technique, they typically describe several benefits, including getting more out of positive situations, appreciating events, and noticing the good even on difficult days.

Is there anyone who couldn't use lots more happiness in their lives? Of course not!

Dr. Delizonna goes on to say another key practice is *savoring*. Savoring is pausing to notice, consider, feel and expand the positive circumstances and experiences that occur. Savor by pausing to relish, soaking in pleasant events as they occur. They "turn up the volume" on fleeting positive events, transforming them into more enduring positive experiences.

These are two powerful techniques because they build habits that reliably create positive emotions, are quick and simple, and require only a shift in focus – no external change is required. And they may just go on to provide you with endless hours of happiness and better health.

Mini-Pumpkin

Whoopie Pies

"Here's the perfect hand-held snack you just won't be able to resist...

Talk about brightening up your dialysis treatment...

Fluffy cream cheese filling sandwiched between two moist pumpkin cookies. Mmm, mmm, mmm!"

Cookies

INGREDIENTS

- ✓ 2 cups all-purpose flour
- ✓ 1 Tsp. baking powder
- ✓ 1 Tsp. baking soda
- ✓ 1 Tsp. ground cinnamon
- ✓ ½ Tsp. ground ginger
- ✓ ½ Tsp. salt
- ✓ ½ cup (1 stick) butter, softened
- ✓ 1 ¼ cups granulated sugar
- ✓ 2 large eggs, at room temperature, lightly beaten
- ✓ 1 cup 100% Pure Pumpkin
- ✓ 1 Tsp. vanilla extract

PREPARATION

1. Preheat oven to 350°F.
2. Lightly grease or line four baking sheets with parchment paper.
3. Combine flour, baking powder, baking soda, cinnamon, ginger and salt in medium bowl.
4. Beat butter and sugar in large mixer bowl on medium speed for 2 minutes.
5. Add eggs, one at a time, beating well after each addition.
6. Add pumpkin and vanilla extract; beat until smooth.
7. Stir in flour mixture until combined.

8. Drop by heaping measured teaspoons onto prepared baking sheets. (A total of 72 cookies are needed for the recipe.)
9. Bake for 10 to 15 minutes or until springy to the touch. Cool on baking sheets for 5 minutes; remove to wire racks to cool completely.

Cream Cheese Filling

INGREDIENTS

- ✓ 4 ounces cream cheese, at room temperature
- ✓ 6 Tbs. butter, softened
- ✓ ½ Tsp. vanilla extract
- ✓ 1 ½ cups powdered sugar

PREPARATION

1. Beat cream cheese, butter and vanilla extract in small mixer bowl on medium speed until fluffy.
2. Gradually beat in powdered sugar until light and fluffy.
3. Spread a heaping teaspoon of filling onto flat side of one cookie; top with flat side of second cookie to make a sandwich. Repeat with remaining cookies and filling.
4. Store in covered container in refrigerator.
5. Yields 3 dozen mini pies.

6. Wrap individually and freeze for up to 3 weeks.

Apple Brie Pizza Bites

"Who said you can't eat pizza any more on a renal diet? Wrap these bites up individually or put a few in an air-tight container to stay fresh or freeze up to a month.

They're crunchy and delicious cold or soft and gooey when quickly warmed up in a toaster oven.

Who doesn't love pizza anytime?"

INGREDIENTS

✓ 1 Refrigerated dough pizza crust

- ✓ 7 oz. brie cheese, with rind, softened
- ✓ 2 tbsp. sour cream
- ✓ ¼ tsp. dill weed
- ✓ 1 tsp. apple juice
- ✓ 1-2 medium red apples, with peel, cut into paper-thin wedges
- ✓ 2 tsp. grated parmesan cheese
- ✓ Black cracked pepper to taste

PREPARATION

1. Prepare and bake refrigerated pizza dough according to package directions.
2. Cool.
3. For topping, mash Brie cheese, sour cream, dill weed, pepper and apple juice with fork on large plate. No need to mash until smooth but rather to coarsely mix.
4. Spread on cooled pizza crust.
5. Arrange apple slices in single layer over spread.
6. Sprinkle with Parmesan cheese.
7. Bake in center of 450°F oven for about 5 min. until crust is crisp and surface is beginning to turn golden.

Broccoli Dip/Crackers

"When your kidneys fail to work properly, you may develop high levels of phosphorus --- a mineral that, along with calcium, supports bone health. To prevent complications of high-phosphorus levels, such as calcium deficiencies and weak bones, your doctor may recommend a low-phosphorus diet.

To maintain a low-phosphorus diet, the Wisconsin College of Medicine suggests limiting high-phosphorus foods, such as peanut butter, nuts, cheese, sardines, chicken liver, beef liver, caramels, beer, ice cream and cola-flavored soft drinks.

Low-phosphorus alternatives to these foods include broccoli, sorbet, zucchini squash, hard candies and non-cola-flavored soft drinks."

INGREDIENTS

- ✓ 10 oz. pkg. frozen broccoli, chopped
- ✓ 1 cup low-fat sour cream
- ✓ ½ cup low-calorie mayonnaise
- ✓ 2 tbsp. green onion, chopped, including tops
- ✓ 1 tbsp. dried parsley
- ✓ ½ tsp. dill weed
- ✓ 1 tsp. garlic powder
- ✓ ¼ cup red bell pepper, chopped

PREPARATION

1. Thaw broccoli, squeeze out excess moisture with paper towel. Finely chop broccoli.
2. In small bowl, combine sour cream and mayonnaise, blend well. Stir in broccoli and remaining ingredients.
3. Refrigerate at least 2 hours.
4. Dip into salt free crackers.

ScrambledEggMuffins

"These are not your boring, ordinary muffins. They're made with plenty of eggs, a little milk, cheese substitute, a little flour, basil and plenty of veggies.

You can make standard sized muffins or spoon the batter into little mini cups for a delightful renal snack!"

INGREDIENTS

- ✓ 9 Eggs
- ✓ ½ cup Chopped fresh spinach
- ✓ 1/3 cup Skim milk or milk substitute
- ✓ 1/3 cup Your favorite baking flour
- ✓ ¼ cup 2% Grated cheddar cheese (or substitute)
- ✓ 1 Tbs. Chopped fresh basil
- ✓ 1 Small tomato chopped
- ✓ ½ cup Yellow/orange bell pepper, chopped
- ✓ ½ cup Fresh kale, chopped
- ✓ Salt & pepper to taste

☼ Quick Tips & Tricks

Try Spelt flour – a popular non-wheat flour that shows up in pastas, breads and in a variety of specifically wheat-free recipes. It has a nutty and slightly sweet flavor and a fairly strong nutritional profile. It is pretty critical not to over mix it, or risk having a crumbly texture imparted into whatever you're making.

PREPARATION

1. Preheat 350®.
2. Break the eggs into a bowl and whisk.

3. Add the rest of your ingredients and mix it all together.
4. Add spoonful's of the mixture to a nonstick muffin tin or a tin sprayed with nonstick coating. I use an ice-cream scoop to transfer the mixture evenly.
5. Pop them in the oven and bake for 25 – 30 minutes, or until well done and golden brown.
6. You can wrap them individually and store in the freezer for up to 3 weeks.
7. Reheat in the microwave for a delicious snack anytime!

Mexican Munchie

Nibblers

"This is a terrific snack to take with you wherever you go... and the extra protein is just an added benefit to the great taste."

INGREDIENTS

✓ 1 egg white, room temperature

- ✓ 2½ tsp. chili powder
- ✓ ½ tsp. cumin
- ✓ ¼ tsp. garlic powder
- ✓ 3 cups Life Cereal® cereal or another corn square type cereal

PREPARATION

1. Beat egg white until foamy.
2. Combine next 3 ingredients in bowl, stir well; fold into egg white.
3. Add cereal, stir gently to coat.
4. Spread mixture on lightly greased cookie sheet.
5. Bake at 325°F for 15 minutes, stirring every 5 minutes.
6. Cool on cookie sheet.
7. Store tightly covered.
8. Makes 6 munchie cups of nibblers!

Nuts & Bolts for

Kidneys

INGREDIENTS

- ✓ 4 cups Cheerios® (or similar substitute)
- ✓ 4 cups Shredded Wheat® (or similar Substitute) cereal
- ✓ 1 cup pretzel sticks
- ✓ 2 cups white bread, cut in cubes
- ✓ ¼ cup margarine, melted
- ✓ ½ cup oil

✓ ½ tsp. garlic Powder
✓ 1 tsp. onion Powder
✓ ¼ tsp. black Pepper

PREPARATION

1. Place white bread on a cutting board, cut in cubes.
2. In a large bowl, mix together bread cubes, and cereals.
3. In a small bowl, melt margarine and pour over cereal mixture.
4. Add oil and spices and stir well.
5. Spread mixture onto 2 cookie sheets.
6. Bake at 250°F for 1 hour.
7. Cool, add pretzel sticks and store in a covered container.
8. Makes 20 – ½ cup servings. Great to take with you just about anywhere. Enjoy!

Kidney-Friendly Bran Muffins

"Did you know that the two main causes of chronic kidney disease are diabetes and high blood pressure? Eating right can go a long way to controlling these diseases."

INGREDIENTS

- ✓ ¼ cup oil
- ✓ 1 egg
- ✓ 1 Tsp. vanilla

✓   1/3 cup honey
✓   1 cup applesauce or crushed pineapple, drained
✓   1 cup white flour
✓   1 cup wheat bran
✓   1 ½ Tsp. baking soda
✓   ¼ Tsp. cream of tartar

PREPARATION

1. Preheat oven to 400ºF and lightly grease muffin tins.
2. MIX: ¼ cup oil, 1 egg, 1 tsp. vanilla, 1/3 cup honey, 1 cup applesauce or crushed pineapple drained.
3. ADD: 1 cup white flour, 1 cup wheat bran, 1 ½ tsp. baking soda, ¼ tsp. cream of tartar.
4. Mix together, spoon into muffin tins and bake immediately. Cream of tartar and baking soda will only rise once so do not delay getting the muffins into the oven.
5. Bake for 15-20 minutes.
6. Makes 12 muffins

Delectable Fruity Rice Pudding

"Use leftover white rice as a head start for this pudding. About 3 cups of cooked rice is equivalent to 1 cup uncooked. "

INGREDIENTS

- ✓ 1 cup non-fat milk (or substitute)
- ✓ 2 cups water
- ✓ 1 can (14 oz.) diced pineapple, sugar free
- ✓ 1 cup sliced strawberries
- ✓ 1 can Mandarin oranges

- ✓ 1 cup blueberries
- ✓ 1 pkg. JELL-O Strawberry Flavor Gelatin (4-serving size)
- ✓ 1 cup instant white rice (uncooked)
- ✓ 1 tsp. ground ginger
- ✓ 1 tsp. grated orange peel
- ✓ 2 cups Cool Whip® Light (or substitute)
- ✓ cinnamon (optional)

PREPARATION

1. Place fruit in 2-qt. bowl; refrigerate until ready to use.
2. Bring 1/3 cup of the juice from canned fruit to boil in small saucepan; pour into large glass measuring cup.
3. Stir in dry gelatin mix 2 min. or until dissolved.
4. Add enough cold leftover fruit juice to measure 1 cup total.
5. Pour over fruit; keep refrigerated.
6. Meanwhile, place 2 cups water and rice in medium saucepan.
7. Bring to boil on medium heat; cover.
8. Simmer 20 min. or until water is absorbed and rice is tender.
9. Stir in milk, sugar and grated orange peel; cook on medium-low heat 5 min. or until creamy, stirring constantly.
10. Cool completely. Gently stir in whipped topping.
11. Spoon rice pudding over fruit and serve or store individually a few days. Garnish with additional fruit and/or cinnamon, if desired.

Roasted Red Pepper

Pizza

INGREDIENTS

- ✓ 1 Greek style pita
- ✓ 2 Tbsp. roasted red pepper sauce (your favorite brand)
- ✓ ¼ cup cooked ground beef
- ✓ 3 slices red pepper
- ✓ 1 Tbsp. onion, diced

✓ 2 Tbsp. brie, diced
✓ 2 Tbsp. mozzarella, grated

PREPARATION

1. Preheat oven to 350°F.
2. Place pita on baking sheet and spread roasted red pepper sauce on pita. Top with beef, red peppers, onion and cheeses.
3. Bake for 10 minutes or until cheese has melted and pizza is heated through.
4. Make up a batch and keep them handy in the refrigerator for a delicious handy snack!

Chicken Finger

Dippers & Dill Sauce

INGREDIENTS

- ✓ ¾ cup Panko breadcrumbs
- ✓ 2 Tbsp. parmesan cheese
- ✓ ¼ Tsp. pepper
- ✓ 1 ½ Tsp. dried thyme
- ✓ ¾ Tsp. each garlic & onion powder
- ✓ 4 chicken breast (halves), boneless, skinless (cut into 1" strips)
- ✓ ¼ cup non-hydrogenated margarine, melted

PREPARATION

1. Preheat oven to 400°F.
2. Combine first 5 ingredients. Dip chicken into melted margarine, then coat with mixed ingredients.
3. Place on lightly greased rack on a cookie sheet.
4. Bake 10 minutes, turn and bake 10 minutes more.

Honey Dill Dipping Sauce

- ✓ ½ cup mayonnaise
- ✓ ¼ cup liquid honey
- ✓ ½ tsp. dried dill weed
- ✓ Mix together...   Refrigerate 30 minutes or more.

Golden Potato

Croquettes

"One of my favorite foods – potatoes – is severely restricted on a renal diet because they contain so much potassium. So, what's the best way to reduce potassium in potatoes? By dialyzing...

For the most effective potassium removal, Davita.com suggests potatoes must be cut into small pieces, sliced thin or grated. If boiled at least 10 minutes in a large pot of water, potassium is reduced by at least half the original amount. These potatoes will still contain 100 to 200 milligrams of potassium in a 1/2 cup serving so people on a low-potassium diet are encouraged to pay attention to portion control.

If boiling is not the planned cooking method, potassium may still be reduced by slicing or cutting potatoes into small pieces or grating them and soaking them in a large amount of water at room temperature or warmer for greater potassium removal.

The least effective method of removing potassium is to soak potatoes in the refrigerator, then prepare without boiling first."

INGREDIENTS

- ✓ 4 medium size potatoes, dialyzed
- ✓ ¼ cup butter (or substitute)
- ✓ 1 tbsp. milk (or substitute)
- ✓ Salt & pepper to taste
- ✓ 1 egg, beaten
- ✓ 3 oz. Panko breadcrumbs
- ✓ 1 tbsp. extra-virgin olive oil
- ✓ 1 tbsp. fresh parsley, chopped

PREPARATION

1. Mash potatoes with butter, milk, parsley and salt & pepper.
2. Shape the croquette with your hand and dip in beaten egg.
3. Roll each croquette in the breadcrumbs.

4. Heat oil and when hot, place a few croquettes in at a time. Make sure you have enough room to turn them easily.
5. Fry on all sides until crisp and golden.
6. Serve warm.
7. Makes 4 servings.

BlackBottom Banana Bars

<u>INGREDIENTS</u>

- ✓ ½ cup margarine, softened
- ✓ 1 cup sugar
- ✓ 1 egg
- ✓ 1 Tsp. vanilla
- ✓ 1 ½ cups mashed ripe bananas (about 3)
- ✓ 1 ½ cups all-purpose flour
- ✓ 1 Tsp. baking powder
- ✓ 1 Tsp. baking soda
- ✓ ½ Tsp. salt
- ✓ ¼ cup baking cocoa

PREPARATION

1. In a mixing bowl, cream margarine and sugar.
2. Add egg and vanilla; beat until thoroughly combined.
3. Blend in the bananas.
4. Combine the flour, baking powder, baking soda, and salt; add to creamed mixture and mix well.
5. Divide batter in half. Add cocoa to half; spread into a greased 13x9x2" baking pan.
6. Spoon remaining batter on top and swirl with a knife.
7. Bake at 350 degrees for 25 minutes or until the bars test done. Cool and enjoy.

Zesty Lemon Squares

INGREDIENTS

- ✓ 1 cup flour margarine, softened
- ✓ 1 cup powdered sugar
- ✓ 2 eggs
- ✓ 1 cup sugar
- ✓ ½ Tsp. baking powder
- ✓ ¼ Tsp. salt
- ✓ 2 Tbs. lemon juice
- ✓ ½ Tsp. vanilla
- ✓ 1 ½ Tsp. milk
- ✓ 1 Meyer lemon sliced into wafer thin matchsticks

PREPARATION

1. Combine flour, ½ cup margarine and ¼ cup powdered sugar in bowl, mixing well.
2. Press into bottom of 9" square baking dish.
3. Bake at 325 degrees for 30 minutes.
4. Combine next 5 ingredients in bowl, beating until fluffy.
5. Pour over first layer.
6. Bake for 25 minutes longer.
7. Cool thoroughly.
8. Combine remaining ¾ cup powdered sugar with 1 tablespoon margarine, vanilla and milk in small bowl, blending until smooth.
9. Spread glaze over lemon layer.
10. Cut into squares and top each slice with curled Meyer lemon matchstick.
11. Out of this world delicious!

Stir-Fried Squash

Vine Tips

"According to LiveStrong.com, the plant Trigonella foenum-graecum, more commonly known as fenugreek, produces seeds useful as a spice and as an herbal remedy for various conditions. Fenugreek has a role in the traditional medicinal system of India, and has long been used for health purposes throughout the Middle East. Fenugreek capsules containing ground seeds are available at many health food & grocery stores.

As a spice, whole or powdered fenugreek seed adds a distinct flavor to curry powders, pastes, sauces and an extra zest to vegetable dishes.. When using dried seeds, lightly roast them before adding them to recipes, advises the Epicentre Encylopedia of Spices."

INGREDIENTS

- ✓ 1 pound pumpkin vine tips, washed, peeled, cut into 1-in. pieces
- ✓ 3 dried red chilies
- ✓ 1 Tsp. fenugreek seeds
- ✓ 1 Tsp. mustard seeds
- ✓ 1 Tsp. cumin seeds
- ✓ 1 Tsp. whole timur (szechwan pepper)
- ✓ 1 Tbs. garlic, minced
- ✓ 1 Tbs. ginger, minced
- ✓ 1 Tsp. cumin powder
- ✓ ½ Tsp. turmeric
- ✓ ½ Tsp. freshly ground pepper
- ✓ 3 Tbs. clarified butter
- ✓ Salt to taste
- ✓ 1 cup chicken or vegetable broth

PREPARATION

1. In a non-stick pan heat 3 tablespoons of clarified butter.

2. Saute fenugreek seeds, whole timur mustard seeds, and cumin seeds until they turn dark.
3. Fry dried red chilies for 15 sec. till they turn dark.
4. Add garlic, ginger, ground pepper, cumin, and turmeric; fry for 1 min in low heat.
5. Add squash vine tips to the spice-mixture, and stir-fry for about 2 min.
6. Salt it to taste.
7. To the stir-fry mixture, add broth, and let simmer until the vine tips are tender and the excess liquid has evaporated off.
8. Adjust seasoning with salt and pepper.
9. Serve with rice or let cool and put them in a bowl to much like nuts.

Power Blueberry

Snacks

"This is a snack recipe first published in the Washington Post, May 21, 2008. Easy enough for kids to make, letting the dough rest will make kneading the dough much easier."

INGREDIENTS

- ✓ 1 ½ cups flour, plus more for the work surface
- ✓ 1 cup Spelt flour (or other whole-wheat flour substitute)
- ✓ 1 Tsp. baking powder
- ✓ ¼ Tsp. freshly grated nutmeg
- ✓ ¼ Tsp. ground cinnamon
- ✓ ½ Tsp. salt
- ✓ 4 Tbs. (½ stick) unsalted butter, melted (or substitute)
- ✓ 1 cup nonfat milk (or substitute)
- ✓ ¾ cup spreadable blueberry fruit (in the jam section of the grocery store)
- ✓ ½ cup frozen blueberries, defrosted or fresh blueberries
- ✓ 1 large egg white
- ✓ 1 tablespoon water
- ✓ ¼ cup wheat germ

PREPARATION

1. Preheat the oven to 350 degrees.
2. Lightly grease a rimmed baking sheet with nonstick cooking oil spray or line with parchment paper.
3. Lightly flour a work surface.
4. Combine the flours, baking powder, nutmeg, cinnamon and salt in a large mixing bowl.
5. Add the melted butter and milk, stirring to form a dough.
6. Transfer dough to the prepared work surface and let it rest for 15 minutes.

7. Then knead the dough for 4 minutes to 8 minutes, until it is smooth and supple.
8. Use a rolling pin to roll the dough into a rectangle that is 12 by 16 inches and 1/2 inch thick.
9. Cut into twelve 4" squares.
10. Spread each dough-square with 1 tablespoon of the blueberry fruit, leaving a clear 1/4-inch margin around the edges of each square.
11. Sprinkle each square with 5 or 6 blueberries.
12. Combine the egg white and water in a small cup to make an egg wash; use a brush to paint the egg wash on the margins.
13. Fold each square in half diagonally to form triangular turnovers.
14. Press down well to seal.
15. Use the tines of a fork to reinforce the seal by pressing along all sides.
16. Lightly brush the tops of the turnovers with the egg mixture.
17. Place turnovers 2 inches apart on the baking sheet.
18. Sprinkle the tops with the wheat germ.
19. Bake about 20 minutes or until golden brown.
20. Transfer to the stovetop (off the heat) and let them cool for 10 minutes before serving.
21. Makes 12 turnover snacks you can wrap individually and store in the refrigerator for up to a week.
22. A delicious dialysis snack!

Cheese Cookie Snack

"From the November, 2001, issue of Southern Living, this snack is a crunchy and satisfying way to get through a treatment or enjoy while reading your favorite book!"

INGREDIENTS

- ✓ 1 cup (4 ounces) shredded Sharp Cheddar cheese (or substitute)

- ✓ ½ cup unsweetened butter (or substitute), softened
- ✓ 1 cup all-purpose flour
- ✓ ¼ tsp. salt
- ✓ 1 cup crisp rice cereal

PREPARATION

1. Stir together cheese and butter until blended. Stir in flour and salt; blend well.
2. Stir in cereal. (Dough will be stiff.)
3. Shape dough into 1" balls; place on an ungreased baking sheet 2 inches apart.
4. Flatten cookies to ¼" thickness with a fork, making a crisscross.
5. Bake at 350° for about 20 minutes or until golden brown.
6. Remove to wire rack to cool. Store in an airtight container.

Bruschetta and Spring Pesto with Peas & Mint

INGREDIENTS:

- ✓ 3 cups frozen peas, defrosted
- ✓ ¼ cup fresh mint leaves
- ✓ 2 hard-boiled eggs, sliced

- ¼ cup Parmesan cheese, grated
- 2 garlic cloves
- ¼ cup pine nuts, toasted
- 1 Tsp. kosher salt
- ¼ Tsp. ground black pepper
- 2 Tbsp. water
- ¾ cup extra virgin olive oil
- Baguette (French or Sourdough)

PREPARATION

1. Add all the ingredients (except the olive oil and boiled eggs) to a food processor and pulse to combine.
2. With the processor running, gradually add the olive oil. Continue to process until puréed to your desire.
3. Depending upon on you prefer to eat it, slice the baguette into ¾" slices and serve either toasted or untoasted.
4. Spread a little pesto over the bread, top with a slice of the boiled egg followed by another dollop of pesto and a few fresh peas for garnish. Enjoy these outrageously delicious and kidney-healthy snacks!!
5. Refrigerate or freeze any extra pesto. You can freeze the pesto in ice cube trays and just pop out a pesto cube whenever you need it!

Texas Bowl of Red

INGREDIENTS

- ✓ 2 Tbsp. extra-virgin olive oil
- ✓ 6 pounds boneless beef chuck or shoulder, cut into ¾" cubes
- ✓ 6 cloves garlic, minced
- ✓ 6 Tbsp. chili powder
- ✓ 4 Tsp. ground cumin
- ✓ ½ cup all-purpose flour
- ✓ 2 Tbs. dried oregano
- ✓ 4 14-ounce cans low-sodium beef broth
- ✓ ½ cup masa harina (instant corn flour)
- ✓ Salt & fresh ground pepper to taste

✓ Chopped white onion and sliced, pickled jalapenos, for topping

PREPARATION

1. Heat 1 tablespoon olive oil in a large Dutch oven over medium-high heat. Add half of the beef and cook, stirring until browned, about 4 minutes. Transfer to a plate.
2. Add the remaining 1 tablespoon olive oil to the pot and brown the remaining beef, then return the first batch to the pot.
3. Reduce the heat to medium and stir in the garlic.
4. Combine the chili powder, cumin and flour in a small bowl. Sprinkle over the meat in the pot and stir until evenly coated.
5. Crumble in the oregano with your fingers, then add 3 cans beef broth, 2 teaspoons of salt and ¼ teaspoon pepper; stir to combine.
6. Bring to a boil, then reduce the heat to low; partially cover and simmer until the meat is just tender, about 90 minutes.

7. Whisk the remaining 1 can broth with the masa harina in a bowl to make a creamy paste; stir into the chili.
8. Continue simmering over low heat until the meat is almost falling apart, about another 60 minutes – adding up to 2 cups water if the chili gets too thick.
9. Serve in bowls topped with onion and pickled jalapenos or as a dip with tortilla chips.

Courtesy Scott Zublin, Texas Chili Parlor, Austin, Texas

Sandwiches

Grilled Paneer

Sandwich

"This is a delicious twist on your traditional 'grilled cheese sandwich' that is everyone's favorite but not exactly a part of the renal diet.

I've modified this wonderful grilled Paneer sandwich from Sailu's Kitchen for a special morning meal or brunch along with a glass of chilled juice or smoothie. It's extremely flavorful and a filling sandwich."

INGREDIENTS

- ✓ 3 Slices of thickly sliced Paneer (or your preferred cottage cheese)
- ✓ 2 tbs. Green chutney
- ✓ 1 tbs. Non-fat yogurt
- ✓ 1 cup Sharp cheddar cheese (or substitute)
- ✓ ½ Red bell pepper cut into thin rings
- ✓ ¼ tsp. Chaat masala (or your preferred Indian spice)
- ✓ 1 cup Grilled onions
- ✓ Salt and pepper to taste
- ✓ 6 Slices sourdough breat
- ✓ Optional: tomato and cucumber slices & lettuce leaves

PREPARATION

1. Marinate paneer slices with 2 tbs. of green chutney (see next page for the recipe), a tbs. yogurt, ¼ tsp. chaat masala, salt and pepper to taste for 30 minutes.
2. Grill them for 10 minutes on medium-high heat or pan roast in 2-3 tsp. of oil until golden brown.

3. Place grilled paneer slices and grilled onions and cheddar cheese on sourdough bread that is buttered on one side.
4. Place on grill (I love a George Foreman for them) and top with another slice of buttered bread on top – grill until brown and bubbly – about 4-5 minutes.   Serve warm.
5. If you wish, arrange lettuce leaves, red bell pepper rings, tomato slices and cucumber slices on the sandwich before serving warm.

Green (Hari) Chutney

"Apart from sweet chutney, another essential item to assemble many Indian meals is Green aka Hari Chutney, prepared with coriander leaves, pudina (mint leaves) and lemon juice.

Quick and simple to make, it can be refrigerated or frozen for many weeks. The chutney will retain its green color due to addition of lemon juice. Hari chutney is versatile and can also be served as a dip or as a spread for many sandwiches."

INGREDIENTS

- ✓ 2 cups chopped fresh coriander leaves, packed
- ✓ 1 cup fresh pudina/mint leaves, packed
- ✓ 2-3 green chilies (adjust to satisfy your own taste)
- ✓ 2 tbs. lemon juice
- ✓ 2 tbs. water
- ✓ 1 ½ tsp. sugar
- ✓ pinch of salt

PREPARATION

1. Wash fresh mint (pudina) and coriander leaves thoroughly and allow the water to drain.
2. Grind the mint and coriander leaves, salt, sugar, lemon juice and green chilies to a fine paste, by adding 2 tbs. water.
3. Remove into a bowl.
4. Refrigerate until use. Works great in hot snacks or as a spread for a sandwich.
5. Pour into ice cube trays and freeze. Wrap individually and use as needed!

Chicken Roti Rolls

"For a snack during dialysis, I prepare roti rolls with different fillings. You can make your own roti (Indian parantha bread) or purchase it premade at your local grocery store where it's readily available. I find the roti a nice change from more traditional tortilla wraps. The roti is a softer and fluffier wrap with a nutty flavor.

When I cook chicken, I usually cook enough to have leftovers that I can slice or shred as need be for the next day's meals or to freeze for future meals. Do the same with turkey. You can be as creative and inventive as your heart desires.

Do yourself a favor when you make them up – make an extra few for a snack later! They taste great hours later, or even in the morning after being refrigerated."

INGREDIENTS

For parantha: (many grocery stores offer packages of pre-made parantha)

- ✓ 1 cup Speltflour (see page 22) or other substitute for whole wheat flour
- ✓ 3/4 cup all-purpose flour
- ✓ 1/2 tsp. salt
- ✓ water to knead the dough
- ✓ oil as required to roast rotis

For chicken filling:

- ✓ 2 cups cooked chicken (chopped or shredded)
- ✓ 2 onions, chopped & mashed to paste
- ✓ ½ tsp. ginger-garlic paste
- ✓ 1 tomato, finely chopped
- ✓ 1 tsp. red chili powder (adjust to your taste)
- ✓ 2 eggs, beaten
- ✓ juice of one large lemon
- ✓ 2-3 onions, finely sliced
- ✓ few tbs. green chutney (see recipe on pg. 25)
- ✓ 2 tbs. olive oil

✓ salt to taste

PREPARATION

1. *If you have pre-packaged parantha, skip ahead to #3.*
   Add salt to the wheat flour substitute and all-purpose flour, combine, slowly add water to form a soft yet slightly firm dough.
2. Cover and let it rest until you get the stuffing ready.
3. Heat olive oil in a pan, add the onion paste and cook for 7-8 minutes over medium heat.
4. Add ginger garlic paste and stir fry for another 3 minutes.
5. Add the tomato and shredded chicken - cover and cook on low flame for 8-10 minutes. Remove from heat.
6. Squeeze lemon juice to taste - then add a little salt and chili powder to taste.
7. On a separate plate, combine the raw sliced onions with 2-3 tbs. of green chutney and keep aside.
8. Beat eggs in a bowl – add salt and pepper and keep aside.
9. To prepare rotis, pinch a large lemon-sized ball of dough, dust the working

surface with some all-purpose flour and roll out the stuffed dough to form 6"-7" diameter circles.
10. Pre-heat your oiled frying pan/grill and cook each parantha lightly on both sides. Prepare all the rotis and place them in a casserole to keep soft.
11. When you are ready to serve them, drizzle some oil on your pan/grill.
12. Fry the roti on one side and on the other side (top) pour 2 tbs. of the beaten egg and flip over the roti so that the egg gets cooked.
13. Remove and place on a plate – place the egg coated side of the roti up and sprinkle some lemon juice on the egg coated side.
14. Place some chicken filling on one end of the roti and sprinkle the onion-green chutney filling and roll the roti tightly to form a roll. To serve, wrap the lower part of the rotis in foil or tissue.
15. Share and Enjoy!

Hot & Spicy Stuffed

Tuna Rolls

INGREDIENTS

- ✓ 4 small, 3" round sourdough bread rolls
- ✓ 2 tbs. low-fat sour cream
- ✓ 2 tbs. reduced-fat mayonnaise
- ✓ 1 tsp. hot chili sauce
- ✓ 2 tsp. fresh lime juice
- ✓ 1 can (6 ounces) tuna in spring water,
- ✓ drained
- ✓ 1 can (8 ounces) corn, drained
- ✓ 1 cup red grapes
- ✓ ½ green pepper, seeded and diced

- ✓ 2 tbs. chopped fresh cilantro
- ✓ Salt and pepper to taste

PREPARATION

1. Preheat the oven to 350°F. Slice the tops off the bread rolls and set aside.
2. Scoop out most of the soft interior, leaving a "shell" about 1/2-inch thick.
3. Make the scooped-out bread into crumbs, either with your fingers or using a food processor.
4. Spread ½ cup of the bread crumbs on a baking tray and toast in the oven until dry and crisp, about 10 minutes. Remove from the oven and set aside; leave the oven on.
5. In a medium bowl mix together the sour cream, mayonnaise, chili sauce, and lime juice. Add the tuna, corn, red grapes, green pepper, cilantro, and dried bread crumbs. Season with salt and pepper to taste. Stir carefully.
6. Spoon the tuna mixture into the hollowed-out rolls and replace the lids. Set on the baking tray and cover loosely with foil.
7. Bake for 5 minutes, then remove the foil and bake for an additional 5 minutes to crisp the bread crust. The filling should be warm but not bubbling. Serve immediately.
8. Enjoy any time of the day or night!

Cranberry Crunch

Chicken

INGREDIENTS

- ✓ 2 cups cooked, chicken, diced or shredded
- ✓ 1 large hard-boiled egg, chopped
- ✓ 2 tbsp. onion, diced
- ✓ ¼ cup celery, diced
- ✓ ¼ cup low-fat mayonnaise
- ✓ 1 tsp. fresh lemon juice
- ✓ 1/3 tsp. sugar
- ✓ Black pepper to taste

PREPARATION

1. Dice or shred chicken.
2. Chop egg, onion and celery.
3. Place in a large bowl.
4. Add mayonnaise, lemon juice, sugar and black pepper.
5. Stir all ingredients together.
6. Cover and chill overnight or at least 2 hours before serving.
7. If desired, serve on bread, roll or pita bread with green leaf lettuce.
8. Makes 6 servings

Hearty Thai Slaw Beef

Sandwich

"Vitamin-packed coleslaw enriches flavorful sliced beef to make a hearty, mouth-watering sandwich you can enjoy any time – heated or cold."

- ✓ 2 tbs. tomato paste
- ✓ ½ cup fresh lime juice (about 3 limes)

- ✓ 1 ½ tsp. ground coriander
- ✓ 1 pound well-trimmed flank steak
- ✓ 1 tsp. sugar
- ✓ 1 tsp. salt
- ✓ 1 tsp. red pepper flakes
- ✓ 3 cups shredded green cabbage
- ✓ 2 carrots, shredded
- ✓ 1 red bell pepper, cut into matchsticks
- ✓ chopped cilantro
- ✓ 1/3 cup chopped fresh mint
- ✓ 4 hard rolls, halved crosswise

PREPARATION

1. In shallow glass dish, stir together tomato paste, half the lime juice, and coriander. Add flank steak, turning to coat.
2. Refrigerate for 30 minutes.
3. In large bowl, whisk together remaining ¼ cup lime juice, sugar, salt, and pepper flakes. Add cabbage, carrots, bell pepper, cilantro, and mint; toss well to combine. Refrigerate.
4. Preheat broiler. Remove steak from marinade. Broil 6 inches from heat for 4 minutes per side for medium-rare, brushing any remaining marinade over steak halfway through cooking time.
5. Let stand for 10 minutes. Cut thin, diagonal slices across the grain.

6. To serve, spoon coleslaw on bottom half of each roll. Cover with steak and top halves of rolls. Serves 4.

Meatball Sliders &

Garlic Sauce

"Boy oh boy, is this one good. Scrumptious moist meatballs simmered in garlic sauce then spooned into a standard, toasted dinner roll and surrounded by melted cheese. How hard is your mouth watering already?

It's a slider of sorts...only it's a meatball sandwich instead of a burger! I got the big thumbs up from the all my testers... they absolutely loved them."

- ✓ 1 lb. ground beef chuck
- ✓ ½ lb. ground veal
- ✓ ½ lb. ground pork
- ✓ 2 tbs. parmesan cheese
- ✓ 1 egg, whisked
- ✓ ½ cup chopped fresh spinach
- ✓ ½ cup panko (bread crumbs)
- ✓ 3 tbs. chopped basil
- ✓ 1 tsp. chopped oregano
- ✓ Salt & black pepper (to taste)
- ✓ ½ cup non-fat milk
- ✓ 2 tbs. extra-virgin olive oil
- ✓ Pinch of crushed red pepper
- ✓ ¼ cup milk (or substitute)
- ✓ ½ whole diced onion
- ✓ 1 jar prepared garlic sauce
- ✓ 12 dinner rolls (sliders)
- ✓ 6 slices Provolone cheese cut in half

PREPARATION

1. In a large bowl, gently mix the ground meats with the breadcrumbs, onion, egg and spinach, cheese, salt & pepper, red pepper and the chopped basil, and oregano.
2. Form the meat mixture into golf ball-size meatballs and transfer to a baking sheet. Cover and refrigerate until chilled, about 30 minutes.
3. Meanwhile, bring the garlic sauce to a simmer and cook over moderately low heat until the sauce is slightly thickened, about 10 minutes.

4. In a large skillet, heat 2 tablespoons of olive oil. Brown the meatballs in batches, about 3 minutes per side. Transfer the meatballs to the garlic sauce and simmer until cooked through, about 30 minutes.
5. Slice dinner rolls through the middle and toast both sides.
6. Spoon meatballs and garlic sauce over each roll. Top with ½ slice of Provolone & enjoy!
7. The meatballs and sauce can be cooked up to 2 days in advance. Reheat gently before serving.

Ginger-Asparagus

Chicken Wraps

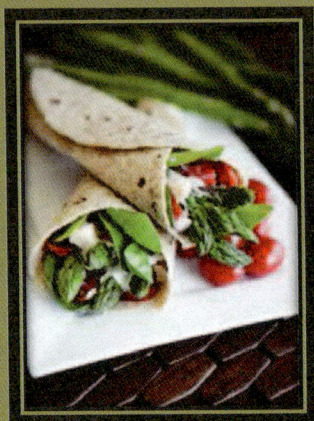

INGREDIENTS

- ✓ 12 asparagus spears
- ✓ ½ cup onion, chopped
- ✓ 2 tbsp. extra-virgin olive oil
- ✓ 2 tbsp. fresh ginger, finely chopped
- ✓ 1 tbsp. hot sauce
- ✓ 2 tbsp. low sodium soy sauce
- ✓ 2 tbsp. brown sugar
- ✓ dash – onion powder
- ✓ 1 lb. chicken, cubed

✓ dash – pepper, to taste
✓ 5 Tortillas

PREPARATION

1. In a large fry pan with lid, add oil, ginger, and onions.
2. Cook covered for 2 minutes.
3. Add asparagus and cook covered for 1 more minute.
4. Combine hot sauce, soy sauce and brown sugar.
5. Pour over vegetables in fry pan and simmer uncovered for 2 minutes.
6. Remove vegetables from pan and set aside.
7. Leave liquid in pan. Add chicken and cook until tender.
8. Add vegetables to chicken and reheat until hot.
9. Spoon mixture into tortillas and enjoy!

Classic Egg-Salad

Sandwich

"Try other mix-ins like sliced black olives, chopped fresh parsley, chopped fresh chives, chopped fresh spinach, chopped dill pickles, and capers."

INGREDIENTS

- ✓ 8 hard-cooked eggs, peeled and coarsely chopped
- ✓ ½ cup mayonnaise
- ✓ 2 tablespoons celery, chopped
- ✓ 2 teaspoons Dijon mustard

- ✓ Few dashes hot-pepper sauce
- ✓ Salt and pepper
- ✓ Lettuce or watercress
- ✓ Bread or toast

PREPARATION

1. In a medium bowl, coarsely chop 8 peeled hard-cooked eggs.
2. Add 1/2 cup mayonnaise, 2 tablespoons chopped celery, 2 teaspoons Dijon mustard, and a few dashes of hot-pepper sauce (or more, if you like a spicier salad).
3. Season to taste with salt and pepper; stir gently to combine.
4. Serve with greens -- such as lettuce or watercress -- on bread or toast.

Adobo Pulled-Pork

Sandwiches

"Pulled pork sandwiches can hardly be called sandwiches. The sauce soaks into the buns and if you tried to pick one up with your hands it would completely fall apart. Well, perhaps if you used a sturdier bun, and wrapped the sandwich in aluminum foil like a burrito, it could be eaten like a sandwich. We just pile the pulled pork on a hamburger bun and eat it with a fork.

*Pulled pork is the perfect slow-cooking winter dish, warm and spicy. This is one of my favorite recipes, and is, in my humble opinion, **the best way to enjoy a dialysis treatment**."*

- ✓ 2 cups drained canned chopped tomatoes
- ✓ 1 tablespoon brown sugar
- ✓ 1 tablespoon chili powder
- ✓ 3 tablespoons red wine vinegar
- ✓ 3 tablespoons adobo sauce
- ✓ 1 tablespoon honey
- ✓ 2 garlic cloves, chopped
- ✓ 4 ½ pounds PORK Shoulder
- ✓ 6 sandwich buns
- ✓ Rosemary-Garlic Mayonnaise (see recipe below)
- ✓ Toppings: lettuce leaves, onion slices

PREPARATION

1. Process first 7 ingredients in a blender or food processor until mixture is smooth.
2. Cut pork in half, and place in a 5-quart slow cooker.
3. Pour tomato mixture over pork.
4. Cook at HIGH for 8 hours; remove from slow cooker.
5. Cool slightly; shred and serve on buns with Rosemary-Garlic Mayonnaise and desired toppings.
6. You can store the adobo pork in an airtight container in the refrigerator for up to a week.

...with Rosemary-

Garlic Mayonnaise

INGREDIENTS

- ✓ ½ cup mayonnaise
- ✓ 2 garlic cloves, minced
- ✓ 1 tablespoon chopped fresh or dried rosemary
- ✓ 1 tablespoon lemon juice
- ✓ 1/8 teaspoon salt

PREPARATION

1. Stir together all ingredients.
2. Chill.
3. Enjoy!!!

Apple-Stuffed Waffle

Sandwich

*"This wonderful recipe from **The Kitchen Diva's Diabetic Cookbook** by **Cass Ryan, Angela Medearis Shelf** (Andrews McMeel Publishing, 2012) makes 4 servings.*

This dual-purpose recipe makes a wonderful breakfast or a tasty snack during any dialysis treatment.

To save time, make the apple topping and the syrup ahead of time, and store them in airtight containers for a week. And, for a delicious variation, use a pear in place of the apple. The syrup also is delicious with other recipes.

INGREDIENTS

- ✓ Apple-Cinnamon Syrup (optional)
- ✓ 2 tablespoons stevia granulated sweetener
- ✓ ¼ cup unsweetened apple juice
- ✓ 1 teaspoon fresh lemon juice
- ✓ 1 teaspoon ground cinnamon
- ✓ 1 crisp red apple (York, Rome Beauty, or Winesap), cored and diced
- ✓ 2 tablespoons stevia granulated sweetener
- ✓ ¼ cup unsweetened apple juice
- ✓ 4 frozen whole-grain waffles or Belgian waffles, toasted
- ✓ 4 tablespoons no-sugar peanut butter (or substitute)

PREPARATION

1. To make the optional apple-cinnamon syrup, place all the ingredients in a small microwaveable bowl and heat on medium (or defrost setting) for 3 to 4 minutes.
2. Cover the bowl with plastic wrap and set aside.
3. In a medium microwaveable bowl, combine the apple, stevia, and apple juice

and cook on high for 4 to 5 minutes, stirring once, until the apple is lightly caramelized and crisp-tender.

4. For each serving, place a waffle on a plate.
5. Spread with 1 tablespoon of peanut butter and 2 tablespoons of the apple mixture. Top with another waffle.
6. Cut the sandwich in half and drizzle with 1 to 2 teaspoons of the apple-cinnamon syrup, if desired.

Made in the USA
Lexington, KY
07 July 2015